Dress to Impress

Calling all aliens!

Are you planning a holiday to planet Earth?

Finn and Zeek are here to help.

'Dress to Impress'
Published by MAVERICK ARTS PUBLISHING LTD

Studio 3A, City Business Centre, 6 Brighton Road,
Horsham, West Sussex, RH13 5BB, +44 (0)1403 256941
© Maverick Arts Publishing Limited May 2019

A CIP catalogue record for this book is available at the British Library.

ISBN 978-1-84886-467-2

www.maverickbooks.co.uk

Credits:
Finn & Zeek illustrations by Jake McDonald, Bright Illustration Agency
Cover: Jake McDonald/ Bright, Hecke61/ Shutterstock
Inside: Shutterstock: Johan Swanepoel (4 & 26), Serban Bogdan (6), Laszlo Mates (8), Suriya99 (8), Muellek Josef (9), Adwo (10), Ktshering (11), Ekaterina Pokrovsky (12), Lukassek (13), Eelnosiva (13), NemesisINC (13), Buritora(14), Supawat Bursuk (15), Troy Rocco (15), JFBPHOTO (16), CRS PHOTO (17), O.C Ritz (18), V. Belov (19),Sirisak Baokaew (20), Diane Diederich (20), Adwo (21), Kzenon (23), Valbunny (24), Vitalinka (25), Don Mammoser (27), Dr. Gilad Fiskus (27), Hecke61 (27)

This book is rated as: Gold Band (Guided Reading)

Dress to Impress

Contents

Introduction	4
Everyday Clothes	8
Hmong Tribe	8
Gho	10
Special Occasions	12
Kilts	12
Kimono	14
The Best of Both	16
Sari	16
Gákti	18
Accessories	20
Hats	20
Beadwork	20
Klompen	26
Quiz	28
Index/Glossary	30

INCOMING MESSAGE

Dear Finn and Zeek,

We want to visit Earth, but we don't know what to wear!

Please can you show us some clothes from different places so that we can be prepared?

From Flim and Flam
(Planet Fashon)

Introduction

America
Scotland
The Netherlands
Bolivia

Humans like to express themselves through the clothes they wear. People around the world have lots of different types of clothes. Throughout the world people dress to impress, whether it is for everyday life or for special occasions.

Everyday Clothes   The Hmong Tribe, Asia

The Hmong people live in East and Southeast Asia. They usually work as farmers or woodcutters. There are lots of different groups to the Hmong, such as the the Black, Striped, White, Flower and Green. These names refer to the colours and patterns of the group's clothes.

Flower Hmong

Black Hmong

The Hmong wear quite basic clothes for every day life such as skirts, trousers and jackets.

Hmong Embroidery

These clothes are **embroidered** in a style which shows which group they come from.

The Hmong are big storytellers. They embroider big sheets of cloth and call them 'story cloths'.

Everyday Clothes   The Gho, Bhutan

In Bhutan, South Asia, the everyday dress for a man is the traditional clothing called the **gho**. This is a robe, worn with a type of scarf called a **kabney**.

The kabney is made of silk and the colour shows the importance of the wearer. Yellow is only worn by the king. Orange is for government ministers and red is for members of the royal family. Green is for judges and blue is for members of parliament. Normal people wear just white.

The women in Bhutan wear a long dress called a **Kira**.

Special Occasions — Kilts, Scotland

The **kilt** comes from Scotland. The kilt is a kind of skirt made from wool, but there's one very unusual thing about it - it is mostly worn by men! In the past, people used to wear kilts all the time. They could be worn a bit like a cloak, covering the whole body. These days, however, most people only wear kilts on important occasions.

The kilt has a criss-cross pattern called **tartan**. Tartan originally was coloured in certain ways to show which clan or family someone belonged to.

A **sporran** is worn with the kilt. This is a handy pouch for keeping things in.

Sporran

Special Occasions — Kimono, Japan

The **kimono** is a robe that is worn in Japan. It reaches to the ankles and has long, wide sleeves. In the past, kimonos were worn every day but they are now mostly worn for special events. The kimono is wrapped around the body with the left side over the right. It is held together with a sash called an obi. This looks like a large bow.

That looks tricky.

Kimonos are usually worn with traditional footwear and socks which have split toes.

The Best of Both   The Sari, India

The **sari** (or saree) is traditionally worn in India and nearby countries. The sari is mainly worn by women. Its name means 'strip of cloth'. It is one long piece of cloth, which can be worn in many different ways. There are over a hundred ways to fold a sari!

Saris are so pretty!

Some saris are very special, and are passed down from mother to daughter. Saris are worn for special occasions as well as in everyday life.

The Best of Both — The Gákti, Sámi

Some traditional clothes are both for everyday and special occasions. One of these is the **gákti**, a type of robe worn by the Sámi people in North **Scandinavia** and Russia.

In the past, the gákti was made from reindeer leather but now it is mostly made with wool, cotton or silk. Most gákti use the colours red, blue, green and white.

It can be very cold in Scandinavia, so the Sámi people's boots, belts and gloves are often made from reindeer skin and fur.

How cosy!

Accessories   Hats

Conical Hats, Asia

Conical hats are found in Asia. They are mostly worn by workers as protection from the sun.

Stetsons, America

Stetsons are known best as cowboy hats. They are waterproof leather hats, which provide shade and, of course, style to the wearer! They were created by John B. Stetson, hence their name.

People around the world wear many different types of hats. Here are a few of them!

Bowler Hats, Bolivia

Bolivian women often wear bowler hats. This fashion started nearly 100 years ago. British men were working on the railway in Bolivia, and a hat-seller ordered a lot of bowler hats which he hoped to sell to the men. But the hats were too small. Luckily for the seller, the little bowler hats became very fashionable for Bolivian women - and they still are today!

Accessories   Maasai Beadwork, Kenya

The Maasai tribe in Kenya has been making bead jewellery for a very long time. At first, the jewellery was made from clay, wood and bone. Glass beads are now more popular. Only women of the tribe are allowed to make the jewellery.

All of the colours and patterns mean something. More colourful jewellery shows that you are more powerful and the shape can show whether you are married or not. Red, blue, green, orange, yellow, white and black are the only colours used and each have their own meaning.

Red - bravery and unity
White - health, peace and purity
Blue - the colour of the sky and energy
Green - the colour of grass and fertility

Black – the people and the struggles they must face

Yellow – the sun, growth and hospitality

Orange – warmth, generosity and friendship

Accessories

Klompen, The Netherlands

Klompen (or clogs) are the national footwear of the Netherlands.

Clogs were worn by both men and women when at work on farms, mines or building sites. They were warm and gave protection to the whole foot. Then when they wore out they could be put on the fire!

They are not worn that often anymore. However, you may still see them being worn by farmers or gardeners.

I think I'll stick with my trainers.

MESSAGE SENT

Dear Flim and Flam,

We have had a colourful tour of different countries and their costumes. Humans have a brilliant imagination! Their clothes are all so different.

Zeek has included a few of her favourite photos for you all, taken with her human camera. What fun!

From,
Finn and Zeek x

Quiz

1. What colour is the most important for a Kabney?
a) Pink
b) Blue
c) Yellow

2. What does the name 'sari' mean?
a) A strip of cloth
b) A hat
c) A large bow

3. What is this Scottish pattern called?

4. Who wears these shoes?
a) The Sámi
b) The Japanese
c) The Hmong

5. Why do workers wear conical hats in Asia?
a) For the colour
b) For warmth
c) For protection from the sun

6. What happens to clogs when they are worn out?
a) They are painted
b) They are put on the fire
c) They are put in the garden

Turn over for answers

Index/Glossary

Embroidered pg 9
When something is decorated with needlework.

Gákti pg 18
Worn by the Sámi people in North Scandinavia, this robe is made to be very warm in the cold conditions.

Gho pg 10
This traditional robe is worn everyday by men in Bhutan, South Asia.

Kabney pg 10-11
A type of scarf worn with a gho robe. The colour of the kabney shows what rank the wearer is.

Kilt pg 12-13
A kind of skirt made from wool worn by men in Scotland, UK.

Kimono pg 14-15
A traditional Japanese robe worn mainly on special occassions.

Quiz Answers:

1. c, 2. a, 3. Tartan, 4. a, 5. c, 6. b

Klompen pg 25

The Dutch word for 'clogs', which are wooden shoes.

Maasai Beadwork pg 22-23

Coloured jewellery made from glass, clay, wood and bone worn by the Maasai tribe, Kenya.

Sari (or saree) pg 16-17

A long piece of cloth from India, which can be worn in many different ways.

Scandinavia pg 18

A region that includes the countries Denmark, Norway, Sweden and Finland.

Sporran pg 13

A pouch for keeping things in, worn with a kilt.

Tartan p 13

A criss-cross pattern used on kilts.

Book Bands for Guided Reading

The Institute of Education book banding system is a scale of colours that reflects the various levels of reading difficulty. The bands are assigned by taking into account the content, the language style, the layout and phonics. Word, phrase and sentence level work is also taken into consideration.

Maverick Early Readers are a bright, attractive range of books covering the pink to white bands. All of these books have been book banded for guided reading to the industry standard and edited by a leading educational consultant.

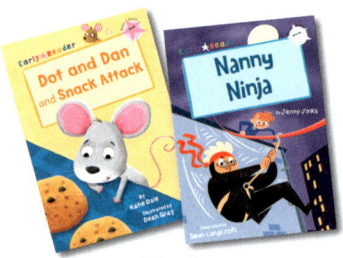

Fiction

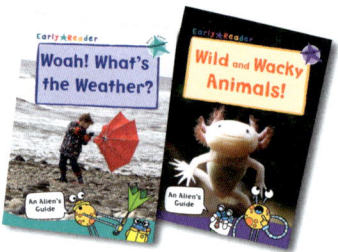

Non-fiction

To view the whole Maverick Readers scheme, visit our website at www.maverickearlyreaders.com

Or scan the QR code above to view our scheme instantly!